NSCIENCE PUBLISHIN(

United Kingdom

nscience publishing house
is part of nscientific services limited
whose addresses can be found at
www.nscience.uk

NSCIENCE

nscience

PUBLISHING HOUSE

Published by nscience publishing house 2020
Copyright © nscience publishing house 2020
Copyeditor: David Fanthorpe
The moral right of the author has been asserted

A CIP catalogue record for this book is available from the British Library

ISBN: 978-1-83853-324-3

'… narcissist… a term specifically coined for the pathology of neurosis.'

C.G. Jung (1922)

CONTENTS

FOREWORD

This book is a distillation of Dr Gwen Adshead's many years of work in the fields of psychiatry and psychotherapy where she has worked extensively with the issues encompassing the whole concept of narcissism.

Looking at narcissism on a continuum from healthy to pathological, Dr Adshead uses research, theoretical ideas and her own extensive clinical experience to delineate and disentangle some of the apparent conundrums in both the concept itself and its cultural context.

Although noting that research in the area is at times contradictory, Dr Adshead brings together what is known about narcissism, stripped of its pejorative implications. This leads to an effective, practical guide for practitioners to evaluate the degree to which the narcissism they may discern in their clinical work is likely to be decisive in the conduct of, and prognosis for, the case before them.

The book contains a section on the key aspects of narcissism, as part of an unhealthy presentation, which is both descriptive and further clarifies for the clinician what to look for and what to take seriously. Dr Adshead points out that there is a paucity of systematic information about this in the psychotherapy profession: although clinicians may have a strong sense of when they may be in the presence of something pathologically narcissistic, this is an intersubjective judgement and often a question of degree. Dr Adshead accordingly provides additional insights to help clinicians towards a sense of perspective and deeper understanding of such cases.

The book goes on to discuss what is known about the causes and origins of unhealthy narcissism in general and narcissistic personality disorder in particular. Again, we are cautioned against easy answers and sweeping generalisations. She notes that unhealthy narcissism is likely to have its roots in infancy and early childhood, when the normal narcissistic stage of development has not, for whatever reason, been successfully navigated;

FOREWORD

and that very often the narcissistic presentation covers its opposite - a fragile and diminished sense of self, which has to be defended against, sometimes at any cost. In the words of the book's title, the self can be deluded and the individual unable to make realistic judgements about themselves or to make plans which take reality into account. This makes it almost impossible for such sufferers to truly learn from experience. It also makes it very difficult for them to form intimate relationships: where there is unhealthy narcissism, there is inevitably a problem in seeing the other as separate, and tolerating that they are different.

Dr Adshead also explores the dynamics of the relationships of the narcissistic person. Noting that this seems often, but not inevitably, to follow gendered lines – with males more likely to exhibit an overt, and females more likely to exhibit a vulnerable, narcissism - she discusses what has been recently called 'echoism'. This is a counterpart to narcissism in which the other person in some way moulds themselves to what the narcissist requires.

Finally, Dr Adshead considers clinical work with people who suffer from the extremes of narcissism. She notes that, as narcissism is understood to be an element of personality, change, if at all possible, will be very slow. The clinician's work is not to return someone to a place of health, pre-crisis or pre-trauma; it is to make something new. Finishing with some thoughts about the challenges for the clinician in this process, Dr Adshead manages to provide a hopeful message which is at the same time profoundly realistic.

Above all, throughout this book is the respectful understanding that the sufferer is just that - suffering. They can also make others suffer with them. Overall thus, this book is an overview, full of insights, of the concept, the condition and the clinical challenges of narcissism.

Dr Jan McGregor Hepburn
London, 2020

INTRODUCTION

The psychological concept of narcissism is complex. Within psychoanalysis and psychotherapeutic thought, there continue to be real debates about which aspects of narcissism might be considered part of the normal spectrum of personality functioning; and what could be considered abnormal or pathological.

The myth of Narcissus is an early psychological 'story' about the tragic consequences for people who fail to recognise themselves, and for the people who love them.

Discussions of narcissism often raise two sets of questions:

- first, questions about what kind of disorder it is; and the extent to which it affects both the self and interpersonal social experience;

- secondly, a question about how and where to set the boundary of normality, and by extension, questions about what therapy might be indicated for abnormal narcissism.

This introduction to narcissism explores these questions, using relevant evidence from the current research literature.

THE NARCISSUS MYTH

Narcissus was the exquisitely handsome son of a nymph. When he was still young, his mother, Liriope, asked the blind seer Teiresias whether her son would live to a ripe old age. Teiresias replied, 'Yes, so long as he never knows himself.'

One day, a nymph called Echo saw him, fell passionately in love with him and pursued him. But when she approached Narcissus, he was horrified and rejected her advances. Narcissus spurned all his other admirers, male and female, until one day a rejected suitor prayed to the gods that Narcissus might fall in love but never obtain his heart's desire. The goddess Nemesis heard the prayer.

One day, Narcissus was out hunting and came, hot and thirsty, to a clear pool. While he was drinking, he was captivated by a vision of beauty that he saw before him. He looked at himself in wonder and then tried to embrace the lovely vision but was always frustrated. He could not tear himself away from the spot, however, until, in the end, he was consumed by the fire of his own passion (or, as some say, took his own life in despair that his passion was unrequited).

This is the version of the story as told in the Roman poet Ovid's Metamorphoses. The Narcissus myth has remained a favourite theme of artists from Caravaggio to Dali and poets from Keats to Heaney.

The idea of narcissism or auto-eroticism has also been a familiar trope of writers, sometimes using terminology reminiscent of the Narcissus myth. For example:

The mythological story of Narcissus is told in subtly different accounts, but essentially contains some key elements of what we now term narcissism:

- it is a disorder of self-recognition;
- it has a disastrous impact on intimate relationships; and
- it brings with it a risk of early death.

'But thou contracted to thine own bright eyes,
Feed'st thy light's flame with self-substantial fuel.'

Shakespeare
Sonnet I, 5-6

Finally, the myth usually ends with the early death of Narcissus by drowning: a reminder that people with narcissistic psychopathology are at increased risk of suicide - just like other people with personality dysfunction.

Early psychologists discussed similar themes though without explicitly referring to the story. The first usage of the name was later claimed by Havelock Ellis, who in an 1898 study of Auto-eroticism, coined the phrase 'Narcissus-like tendency' to describe self-absorption in sexual self-admiration, though he noted that the word 'narcissism' was coined by the German psychiatrist Paul Näcke a year later.

Freud used the term for the first time in writing in 1910, in his Three Essays on Sexuality, prior to his full study, On Narcissism: An Introduction (1914). He also credited his early collaborator Otto Rank with helping to develop the theory of narcissism.

THEORIES OF NARCISSISM 'HEALTHY' NARCISSISM

There are two different theoretical approaches to narcissism, which then generate different kinds of data. The first kind of research is done by social psychology researchers who work mainly in academic settings and who base their research mostly on studies of undergraduate students. These studies find that narcissism is a personality trait which is present in everyone, to a greater or lesser degree; it is seen as an essentially normal trait, which is normally distributed. On this view, having some narcissistic aspects to one's personality could even be advantageous in some social circumstances and environments; for example, in terms of leadership and optimism.

Developmental researchers also argue that there is a kind of 'healthy' narcissism which is a normal part of childhood development; for example, most toddlers present as 'narcissists' in terms of being grandiose, vulnerable, me-oriented and entitled.

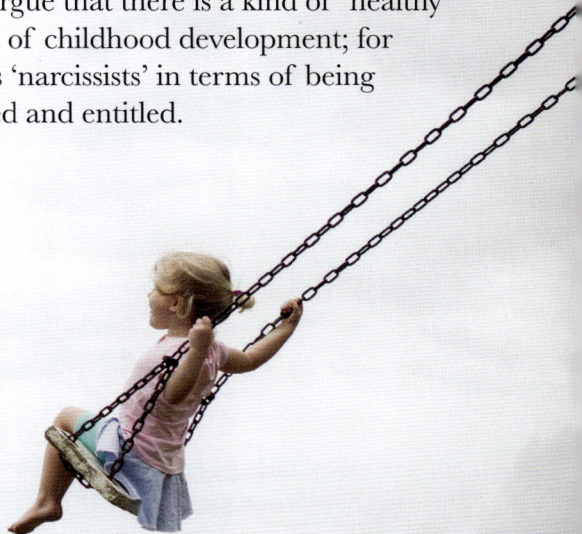

'HEALTHY' NARCISSISM

Normal narcissism might be said to involve a kind of positive belief in the self which could be necessary to good social functioning and which might be an important aspect of the way in which we make boundaries between ourselves and other people. That sense of oneself as being important, or valuable and significant, or notable, or even visible may be part of what helps one to develop a sense of oneself, quite separately from others.

The group analyst *Sigmund Karterud* (2010) has suggested that humans need to develop a strong sense of an individual self in order to distinguish themselves from other members of the social groups to which they belong. Human beings are primates who have to live in groups across their lifespan; and to have a strong sense of self may be important for negotiating social relationships of dominance and status. There may also be elements of normal narcissism that play a significant part in displaying leadership within a group, such as idealism, optimism, self-confidence and the denial of vulnerability.

But if that self-confidence and denial of vulnerability become rigid and entrenched, then this may make dealing with ambiguity and uncertainty difficult, which will have social costs. As previously noted, vulnerability is a key part of most intimate relationships, so what might be a positive aspect of narcissism might also, in certain contexts, be problematic. Issues like this are a reminder that in any discussion of personality traits, context – social context - is crucial.

DEMOGRAPHY

A web-based study suggested that something that looks like narcissism exists almost everywhere, but that there were higher levels of narcissistic tendencies in cultures which have an emphasis on an indexical self as opposed to a referential self, i.e. cultures which emphasise the indexical self-focus on each person as an individual, whose self-experience is defined by them; in contrast, the concept of the referential self is found in cultures that emphasise relationships between people and where people define themselves in terms of their relationship with other people, and the roles they play in their community. The referential self is found most often in eastern cultures; in contrast to most western, anglophone cultures, where people tend to define themselves in isolation from relationships and roles.

In this study, Black and Hispanic individuals scored higher than other ethnic groups, and it is unclear what this means. It may be linked with problems of racism and social exclusion; but it may also be linked with cultural accounts of masculinity. There is a complex relationship between narcissism and gender: traits like 'exploitativeness', entitlement and also leadership may be evidence of narcissism but are also sometimes seen as masculine. This overlap with gender stereotypes may explain why males tend to score higher than females on measures of narcissism. The study also found that scores tend to decrease with age, so the peak years for narcissistic tendencies are perhaps the 30s and 40s.

UNHEALTHY NARCISSISM: THE CONCEPT OF NARCISSISTIC PERSONALITY DISORDER (NPD)

The second kind of research on narcissism is based on work with clinical populations, i.e. on people who seek out professional help for assessment and psychological therapy. Clinicians therefore see a different population from academic researchers. From a clinical perspective, narcissistic personality disorder (NPD) is a pathology of the self with degrees of severity, but which is always pathological. Like other personality disorders, NPD can be highly problematic for individuals and their social interactions; it can co-exist with other mental disorders such as substance misuse and other personality disorders, for example antisocial PD and borderline PD.

Part of the challenge of developing an agreed theoretical model of narcissism is that the theoretical understanding of personality disorder is itself a developing subject. Both the ICD- 11 and the DSM-5 (which define mental diagnoses) describe personality disorder on a spectrum of severity. ICD-11 describes personality dysfunction, as opposed to disorder; it suggests that there are degrees of dysfunction, from mild through moderate to severe. This approach argues for a continuum between the normal and the abnormal; it is clinically helpful insofar as it also supports the idea that the severity of personality disorders might change if people's personal circumstances change.

Table 1

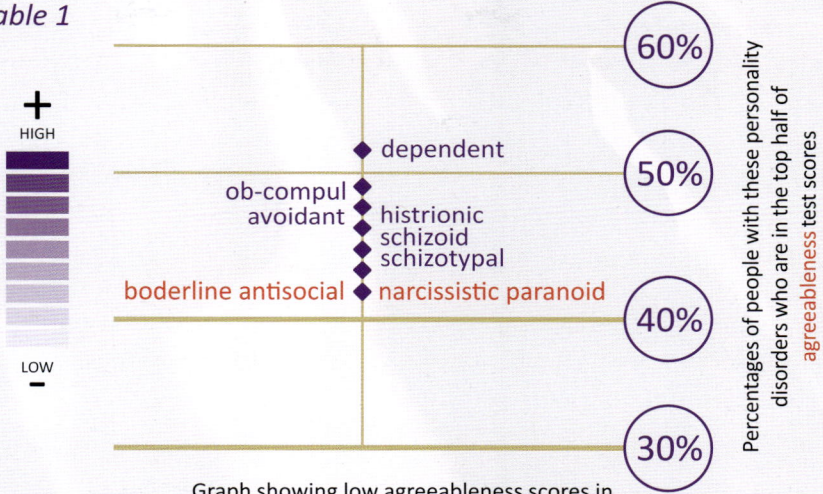

Graph showing low agreeableness scores in
Antisocial, Paranoid and Narcissistic Personality Disorders.

LOW AGREEABLENESS
Are angry or hostile, self-centered and lacking in empathy, and blame others for
their difficulties. Are suspicious of others, and prone to getting into power struggles.
They hold grudges, feel victimized, and elicit animosity.
They lack close friendships.

Adapted from Saulsman, L.M. and Page, A.C., 2004. The five-factor model and personality disorder empirical literature: A meta-analytic review. Clinical psychology review, 23(8), pp.1055-1085.

The Five Factor Model (FFM) of personality states that each person's personality is built around five traits: openness to experience; conscientiousness; extraversion; agreeableness; and neuroticism (OCEAN). One study *(Table 1)* found that narcissism has a close relationship with extraversion but a negative relationship with being agreeable and conscientious. This fits with the idea of pathological narcissism as a disorder of personality, which implies that interpersonal dysfunction is likely to be a major problem for people who are narcissistic.

The next table *(Table 2)* sets out a continuum from ordinary, normal or 'healthy' narcissism to the pathological end of the spectrum. In a way, the table draws some boundaries, but real life of course is not like that. The interesting question for psychotherapists is whether it is possible for people in a severe state of narcissism to become less so with treatment; or whether, like other personality disorders, it is only the mild and moderate degrees of narcissistic PD that respond to treatment. It is also the case that people with severe NPD are unlikely to seek treatment (they're too grand!); and the most risky cases (where NPD is combined with antisocial PD or psychopathy) are thankfully rare in the general population and uncommon even in prisons and secure psychiatric services.

Table 2

Healthy ———————————————— Unhealthy ———————————————— Pathological

NARCISSISM KEY

Healthy Narcissism	Stable Narcissism	Destructive Narcissism	Pathological Narcissism
	Normal Narcissism		Clinical Narcissism
Age Appropiate Narcissism (Kohut; Brown)	Extraordinary Narcissism (Ronningstam)	Destructive Narcissistic Pattern (Brown)	Narcissistic Personality Disorder (DSM)
Cohesive Integrated Self (Kernberg)	Productive Narcissism (Maccoby)	UnProductive Narcissism (Maccoby)	Personality Disorders Cluster B Disorders (DSM)
	Codependency (Whitfield) Co-Narcissism (Rappoport)		Malignant Narcissism
			AntiSocial PD
			Psychopathy
Adaptive Flexible Traits	Semi-Flexible Traits	Semi-Rigid Traits	Rigid Personality Traits
Trait Narcissism	(15.3 average NPI)	++ Entitlement/Exploitativeness	

It is worth repeating that there is still real uncertainty about where to place the boundary between ordinary narcissism (which might be positive and effective), and pathological narcissism (which always causes problems in interpersonal relationships). Psychotherapists and psychoanalysts may feel that in their day-to-day practice they 'know it when they see it'; however, it is much less clear that one can identify NPD that easily. Therapists should be reluctant to 'diagnose' NPD on the basis only of a third-party account, i.e. without actually making their own assessment.

The DSM-5 model provides in some ways a checklist of personality traits which one might ordinarily associate with narcissism:

- grandiosity / arrogance

- fantasies of extraordinary achievement and power, held in the face of the evidence

- focus on status and competition and a need to be admired

- sense of entitlement and associated envy

- lack of empathy / interpersonal exploitativeness

- mood disorder and entitlement rage.

Underlying many of these aspects of narcissism is a sense of vulnerability and fragility, especially a fear of exposure, which is further discussed below.

This issue of entitlement and associated envy felt towards others who may have / be enjoying / have achieved a position, attribute, reward or whatever is interesting, because it hints at narcissistic traits as a kind of distortion of a normal tendency to compare oneself with others, in terms of status and hierarchy. People who live in groups often participate in this kind of comparing activity: we rank ourselves *vis-à-vis* other people, gauging our position in various kinds of hierarchy. It may be that we do this more at certain times than at others (for example in younger age as we develop a sense of self); it is also possible that some people are more prone to envious comparisons than others. The question is, when does that kind of thinking stop being a kind of normally unhelpful thought that one can let go, and when does it become a way of being in the world, which is a significant problem? Of course, this is a question one can ask about many aspects of our minds.

'In my opinion, narcissism is the libidinal complement of egoism.'

Sigmund Freud
On Narcissism: An Introduction (1914)

NARCISSISM, VULNERABILITY AND FRAGILITY

Earlier, we noted that an entrenched denial of vulnerability was one of the aspects of narcissism which makes having healthy relationships problematic. As we have also seen, a contempt for others' vulnerability is a component of the exploitativeness and lack of empathy associated with NPD. Many writers on narcissism in fact see vulnerability and fragility as strongly correlated with pathological narcissism: indeed, one can ask whether it is possible to have the grandiosity of the narcissist without a kind of hypersensitive fragility. It seems in fact that they are two sides of the same coin, or two manifestations of the same problem.

One way of seeking to understand this relationship between grandiosity and fragility has been the development of a distinction between 'thin-skinned' and 'thick-skinned' narcissists, as discussed by *Rosenfeld (1987)*. He argues that there are essentially two types of defence deployed against whatever the perceived deficit is to which the narcissist feels vulnerable: a 'thick-skinned' defence, which is grandiose, exploitative and controlling – this is the 'attack is the best form of defence' approach; and a 'thin-skinned' defence, which is associated with hypersensitivity, the expression of high levels of conscious distress, and anxiety and shame (and probably unconscious anger, even rage). These two different defence mechanisms are, in effect, two social expressions of a self-related problem. Anthony Bateman has also applied this dichotomy to people with borderline personality disorder and discussed the implications for therapists. It is also intriguing to think whether one could describe organisations and even countries as either 'thick' or 'thin-skinned' narcissists.

OTHER WAYS OF UNDERSTANDING NARCISSISTIC DISORDERS

The theoretical underpinning of what constitutes or defines pathological narcissism continues to evolve. Another account of pathological narcissism, by *Russ, Shedler, Bradley and Westen (2008)*, which was based on a sample of patients, discerns three slightly different forms:

- grandiose / malignant narcissism
- vulnerable narcissism
- high-functioning narcissism.

This last leads to the longstanding debate as to whether someone can have a personality dysfunction and yet be socially high-functioning. There are important questions of definition here. Some of those who take up leadership positions in organisations – company chief executives, for example, or politicians – may be described as highly narcissistic and are evidently in one way high-functioning. But of course they may be highly successful at what they do and at the same time have highly unsatisfactory relationships in their life away from work. The answer would seem to be that someone can have a relatively mild personality dysfunction and yet be socially high-functioning.

'Whoever loves becomes humble.
Those who love have, so to speak,
pawned a part of their narcissism'

Sigmund Freud

A more longstanding debate is over whether there is a correlation between narcissism and high levels of self-esteem. That may appear obvious, but it is important to add that the level of self-esteem must be disproportionate to the individual's personal situation: some high-achieving individuals, in the worlds of the arts or sport, for example, may actually need to have high levels of self-esteem in order to perform as they do. Social psychologists have suggested that although many narcissists claim to have high levels of self-esteem, this is in fact only a defence mechanism - a view which would match the classic clinical view. In a study from 2013, *Vater et al.* measured self-esteem in a group of people who scored highly on the narcissistic personality inventory (NPI); and found that individuals with NPD had lower self-esteem than the control group, and they were more depressed. This makes sense if one thinks about narcissism as a kind of defence but rather goes against the idea of a kind of formal pathology of personality.

The DSM-5 model, introduced earlier, also gives a way of assessing the severity of the disorder in an individual. The model suggests looking at five personality traits, but in this case not the five familiar from the Five Factor Model (see above), but five traits – which we all probably have to some degree - from our 'shadow' side:

- **psychoticism** – the tendency to be poor at reality testing

- **antagonism** – the propensity to be disputatious, to be paranoid and aggressive

- **neuroticism** – the inability to deal effectively with painful or challenging emotions

- **dissocial behaviour** – a tendency to break the rules

- **avoidance / detachment** – keeping away from other people and relationships.

The suggestion of this model is that assessing the level of these traits in an individual offers a means of gauging the degree of narcissism displayed by that person.

The challenge of 'calibrating' the severity of narcissistic disorder is one which has attracted a number of proposed solutions. Pincus- *(Pincus and Lukowitsky, 2010)* has developed a pathological narcissism inventory (PNI), which is different from the NPI described above, and is intended to focus only on those people with clinical personality pathology. He suggests that people with NPD oscillate unpredictably between grandiose and vulnerable senses of self, which causes disturbance of mood and problems in relationships. Pincus goes on to argue that the pathological narcissist therefore has problems not only with self-esteem but also with negative affects, in particular rage, hostility and – above all – shame. Shame is a very important part in this context because it is a social emotion, which involves a perception of how others see us. Shame is an emotion that we see in other primates who live in groups with hierarchies; and it is therefore not surprising that it is a big problem for people with narcissistic disorders.

One challenge for any attempt to assess any personality disorder is the extent to which it is possible to rely on self-reported data. In *Vater et al.'s study (2013)*, referred to above, there was little overlap between self-reported symptoms and reported scores using the SCID-II system: people who scored highly on the NPD were not the people whom the SCID 'scorers' rated as narcissistic. It may well be of course that these different measures of personality are simply picking up different aspects of the personality; that our personalities are complex functions of the mind with multiple facets.

Pincus' model of NPD fits well with a psychodynamic model of mind, in which there are emotions that are always moving out of consciousness and unconsciousness and things that are available to the conscious mind, things that are not so available, and defences which work in a similar way. The defence theory of personality structure (that defences are cognitive-affective psychological structures with conscious and unconscious elements that operate in interpersonal social spaces) would say that most personality tests and measures will only pick up the conscious, not the unconscious, defences. To get at those, you need different kinds of assessment: for example, the *Adult Attachment Interview*, although not a formal measure of personality, uses language to explore unconscious ways of thinking about the world and others in it.

Defences operate in the interpersonal space between people; they have an outside and an inside. The difficulty we have, as observers, about defences is that we see the outside of the defence, but the lived experience of the person on the inside of the defence is completely different. What they are experiencing and seeing, for want of a better term, through the lens of their defence is not what observers see on the outside curvature, as it were, of the defence that operates as that boundary. Of course, what they see in others is also quite complicated.

HOW COMMON IS NPD?

A major epidemiological study of around 44,000 people, conducted in the US as part of its National Epidemiologic Survey on Alcohol and Related Conditions (NESARC) and reported by *Stinson et al.* in the *Journal of Clinical Psychiatry* in 2008, concluded that 6.2% of the sample population met the criteria for NPD. The figures for men and women were markedly different: 7.7% as against 4.8%.

As mentioned earlier, the rates for Black and Hispanic groups were higher, which may have something to do with cultural concepts of masculinity. The people who met the criteria for NPD in this study also had high levels of mental disability and high levels of comorbidity with other disorders, including other personality disorders and problems with substance misuse.

'Hate is the complement of fear and narcissists like being feared. It imbues them with an intoxicating sensation of omnipotence.'

Sam Vaknin
Malignant Self-Love: Narcissism Revisited (2001)

The NESARC data also suggested that NPD traits may improve with age, though much depends on how people present: it may be that NPD traits in older populations are to some extent masked by other conditions. There are some very interesting anecdotal data coming out of old age services, where people's declining frontal lobe functions allow a much more pronounced kind of narcissistic deficit to emerge. Something that was hidden by good enough cognitive function may then be revealed as these functions begin to diminish.

Of course, what is not clear is whether the narcissistic disorder was always present, but just well-handled, or whether the disorder is actually made much worse by the falling apart of some of the orbitofrontal cortical connections.

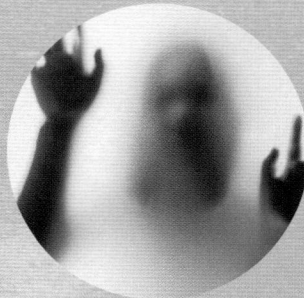

'She is a woman who lives for others.
You can tell the others by their hunted expression.'

C S Lewis has a nice turn of phrase to
describe sacrificing self-enhancement.

A study by *Wright et al. (2013)* found some support for two ways of presenting as narcissistic – the 'vulnerable' and the 'grandiose'. They further found some limited support for a split on gender lines: males tend to present as grandiose and females as vulnerable. Some aspects of pathological narcissism resemble a toxic version of masculine gender role stereotypes: being masterful, ignoring others' views, self-confidence, leadership, being active without being reflective. Again, stereotypical accounts of femininity often have something in common with the vulnerable version of pathological narcissism: victimhood as an identity, other people viewed as active sources of threat, always being vulnerable, neediness, self-sacrifice that's controlling of others. Now of course this dichotomy has to be directed by social gender role modelling, but in this particular study other features were also important, including:

- contingent self-esteem
- exploitativeness
- sacrificing self-enhancement
- devaluing others
- entitlement rage
- hiding the self
- psychosomatic disorders

The concept of sacrificing self-enhancement – the idea that one's self is built around living for other people, looking after other people – is very interesting in relation to women.

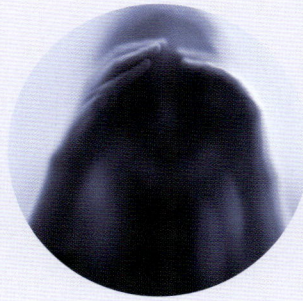

There is some echo here of psychosomatic disorders and other disorders of embodiment, where people struggle to manage distress and vulnerability and tend to express it in a physical, rather than an emotional, way. Such people are often uncomfortable with exploring their self-experience at all; and may rigidly locate their experience in their bodies, always seeking physical treatments that cannot work because the problem is not in the body. Such an approach to emotions can become part of the personality function and can sometimes appear quite narcissistic.

Donna Savary has done some very interesting work on people who become attached to narcissists. She has developed the concept of the 'echoist', who is usually, though of course not always, female, and whose subjective experience of themselves is as empty or absent, a void which is filled by the narcissistic partner. Perhaps what therapy can do for people whose experience of themselves is like this is to help them develop an increased sense of agency. That fits with what we know about effective therapy generally: that nearly all effective therapy does tend to give people a different kind of narrative of agency, particularly around painful or challenging affects.

IS THERE A LINK BETWEEN NPD AND PSYCHOPATHY?

While it is the case that not all narcissists meet the criteria for psychopathy, many psychopaths do meet the criteria for narcissistic personality disorder. But it is important not to assume that there is a correlation between having NPD and the risk of being violent. Lack of empathy by itself is not a risk factor for violent behaviour; conversely, a propensity to violence is associated with multiple risk factors.

'... *a way of life that is dying -*
the culture of competitive individualism,
which in its decadence has carried the logic
of individualism to the extreme of a war
of all against all, the pursuit of happiness
to the dead end of a narcissistic
preoccupation with the self.'

Christopher Lasch
The Culture of Narcissism (1979)

CAUSES OF NPD

The causes of NPD are bound up with the larger question about how someone becomes personality disordered at all. Most of the theories have focused on something going wrong in the early attachment between parents and children. Studies of attachment pathology in narcissists have noted a link with avoidant attachment style; especially avoidance of intimacy and the denigration of vulnerability. These are both features of a kind of dismissing attachment, which denies vulnerability and makes strong claims to strength and normality. Many studies have found a relationship between insecure attachment and personality disorder diagnoses.

Attachment insecurity is also relevant to the issue of mentalising, or metacognitive function, to use different terminology; this is the idea that we are able to keep not only our own minds but also the minds of others in mind. It may be that people with high levels of narcissistic pathology do not see other people as real and certainly do not see other people as having minds like them, or minds that are real, minds that count.

Narcissistic personality disorder seems to involve a fairly drastic failure of mentalising, and it seems unlikely that traumatic stress is going to be a sufficient explanation. Other explanations could include sensitivity to status and hierarchy, and shame, including particular experiences of shame in childhood. There are also studies suggesting that they there may be different patterns of neuronal activity in people with NPD, compared with a control group.

TREATMENT

A key reference on the treatment of people with NPD is *Gabbard and Crisp (2018)*. They underline the fact that treatment is difficult and likely to require a long time. One major initial difficulty is that the usual starting point for therapy is that the patient acknowledges that there is a problem – but this may be very difficult for a person with NPD to acknowledge. As discussed above, it is doubtful that people with NPD are able to reality test effectively. They are likely to be highly antagonistic towards the very notion of therapy. Countertransference is also a particular challenge in the treatment of NPD, because the very process of being in therapy provokes anxiety in the patient. Group work, which might otherwise appear the best option and is widely used in the treatment of Borderline Personality Disorder, is likely to stir up envy and competition; but individual work stirs up pathological dependence and sensitivity to rejection or slight. As part of a long process, it is necessary to start with building up resilience and distress tolerance and then checking that there is a reasonable therapeutic alliance in place.

CONCLUSION

Narcissistic personality disorders continue to puzzle us because they may be discussed in everyday terms of vice and virtue and because they raise questions about the development of the self. There may be subtypes of NPD, though it may be the case that the same pathology expresses in different ways.

Narcissistic personality disorder raises interesting questions about power, control in relationships and vulnerability with others, especially where we have to depend or rely on others for help and support. Discussions about narcissism are also discussions about what it is to have a social self, a relational self; about the boundaries between self and others, and control over relational spaces; and about other minds, the conception of other minds, the comfort and tolerance of letting other minds that are different be in a world, in a space.

Treatment is likely to be prolonged and presents significant challenges. The risk to others is highest if other risk factors for violent behaviours are present; the risk to the patient may be high and may be made worse by treatment.

REFERENCES

Gabbard, G., & Crisp, H. (2018).
Narcissism and its discontents.
Washington, DC: APA Publishing.

Karterud, S. (2010).
On narcissism, evolution and group dynamics:
A tribute to Malcolm Pines.
Group Analysis, 43 (3), 301-310.
doi: 10.1177/2F0533316410372247.

Pincus, A., & Lukowitsky, M. (2010).
Pathological narcissism and narcissistic personality disorder.
Ann Rev Clin Psychol, 6, 421-426.
doi: 10.1146/annurev.clinpsy.121208.131215.

Rosenfeld, H. (1987).
Impasse and interpretation: Therapeutic and anti-therapeutic
factors in the psychoanalytic treatment of psychotic, borderline,
and neurotic patients (pp. 85-104).
London and New York: Tavistock / Routledge.

Russ, E., Shedler, J., Bradley, R., & Westen, D. (2008).
Refining the construct of narcissistic personality disorder:
Diagnostic criteria and subtypes.
Am J Psychiatry, 165 (11): 1473-81.
doi: 10.1176/appi.ajp.2008.07030376.

REFERENCES

Savery, D. C. (2018).
Echoism: The Silenced Response to Narcissism.
London Routledge Books.

Stinson, F., Dawson, D., Goldstein, R., Chou,
S., Huang, B., Smith, S., Grant, B. (2008).
*Prevalence, correlates, disability, and comorbidity of DSM-IV narcissistic
personality disorder: Results of the wave 2 national epidemiologic survey
on alcohol and related conditions.*
J Clin Psychiatry, 69 (7), 1033-45.

Vater, A., Schröder-Abé, M., Ritter, K., Renneberg,
B., Schulze, L., Bosson, J., & Roepke, S. (2013).
*The narcissistic personality inventory: A useful tool for assessing pathological
narcissism? Evidence from patients with Narcissistic Personality Disorder.*
Journal of Personality Assessment, 95 (3), 301-308.

Wright, A., Pincus, A., Thomas, K., Hopwood,
C., Markon, K. & Krueger, R. (2013).
Concepts of narcissism and the DSM-5 pathological personality traits.
Assessment, 20 (3), 339-352.